Rest

Forward

Worship is the most important activity that takes place in our walk with God and in our churches. The whole of the Bible, from the fall of man, through to Revelations, is the story of Gods' plan of redemption for His people. Our worship, our submission to Jesus and His purposes, is central to that.

We were not created to be pastors, evangelists or for any other church activity, (although these have become necessary due to man's rebellion,) we were created for one purpose; that we might be close to Him, to walk with Him, and be intimate with Him, and that we would enjoy Him, and Him us. We are Jesus' bride, we are His desire, and we are His children.

We will never fulfil all that God had for us without intimacy with Him. Being close to Him must be the focal point of both our personal lives, and of our churches, because if He is not the centre, then we have missed the point. It is too easy to become focused upon the things of God, especially those of us in lay or full time ministry, whilst losing our focus upon the true goal, Jesus Himself. Unless we learn how to walk with Him, we will never see the fullness of His restoration in our lives. We may have all the teaching, all the activity, all the professionalism, and yet without Him, we will only have empty religion.

It is for this reason that I have spoken across the globe, teaching on how to draw closer to God, seeing Him become the centre of all we do. Jesus is calling His bride to turn her heart to Him again, to meet Him, and to walk with Him in everything that He has for us.

In this book, I hope to explain what worship is, and how central it is in all that God does with His people from the Old Testament to the New, and how we need to apply His teaching to both our personal lives and our churches.

My passion is that we each grow closer to Him, and that our churches become places full of His glory, power and wonder. If you have any questions about worship, or about the content of this book, feel free to email: ben@worshipacademy.co.uk, or connect with me on Facebook at: www.facebook.com/The.Worship.Centre

Thank you,

Benjamin Sealey

What is worship?

To truly understand worship, we must begin at the very beginning of the Bible.

When God created man, He did so for one reason, because He loved him and wanted to be with him. God desired fellowship with His creation. Because there was no sin in the world, no rebellion, man walked in perfect harmony with God. Man was completely submitted to God, he had no disobedience in his heart, and so because of this both man and God walked together in perfect union.

This was how God intended it be, and how it should always have been, man living in complete submission to, and living in, the fullness of God.

It was out of this place though, that man was seduced into rebelling against God, in Genesis chapter 3. Because of man's sin and rebellion towards God, that unity between them was lost, and man was expelled from the Garden of Eden. The whole of the Bible is the story of God restoring that intimacy between Himself and man. Man could no longer walk with God as he had in the Garden of Eden, because of sin and rebellion. It is because of this, that He sent Jesus to pay the price for that rebellion, that we might know Him once more as God intended.

It is important to understand this background, to fully understand worship, because we must always understand that God's first and foremost desire is that we walk closely with Him again, in complete submission to Him

The English word "worship" literally means worth-ship. It ascribing worth to something. At its' core, the word worship is about surrender. In England, in crown courts, we address the judge as "your worship." In doing so, we are acknowledging that the judge has more worth than us, is a higher authority than us. In worshipping someone, we are lifting them above us, and at the same time, we are surrendering to them.

So our worship to God is our active decision to put aside our own desires and motives, and instead acknowledging God's worth, His authority, His rule and His power. It is both surrendering ourselves, and lifting Him up.

The process of surrendering, as we will see later, is the means by which we draw closer to God. In the Garden of Eden, we lost our relationship with God through our rebellion. Now, through Jesus, when we actively decide to surrender ourselves and seek His worth over our own, we will draw closer to Him.

Worship, therefore, is not actually the goal - it the process by which we achieve the goal. The goal is to encounter God and be close to Him. The process by which we achieve that goal is worship.

To worship or not to worship is always our decision. God wants us to surrender to Him out of love, not because we are forced to. There will be a time when all eyes will see Him, and every knee will bow before Him, but that time is not now. Now is a time for those who would seek Him, for those who would sacrifice their lives for the sake of drawing near to Him. God is not looking for slaves, those who are forced to submit, but servants, those who choose to submit.

It is important to understand that when God talks about worship, He is not talking about music, (although there is a place for music, as we will discover,) or about singing the latest chorus or hymn, He is talking about those who would give their all for Him in complete surrender.

Paul understood this when he wrote, *"Therefore, I urge you, brothers and sisters, in view of God's mercy, to offer your bodies as a living sacrifice, holy and pleasing to God---this is your true and proper worship" (Romans 12:1.)*

He realised that true worship was giving his life as a sacrifice before God, surrendered to His will. This is the true worship that God is looking for in these times, those who would forsake their lives for Him.

If we are to lead God's people into worship, and see powerful, life changing worship in our own lives, and in our churches, we must be completely clear about what worship is, we must understand that we are leading the people into that place of surrender.

All of us must have worship at the centre of our lives and of our churches. God moves wherever we allow Him to, so as we go deeper in our surrendering and our dependency upon Him, He will be able to move in new and more powerful ways.

Most of what God has done in my own life has been in those times of worship, in those places of true encounter. I've experienced the Glory of God like I could not even describe, I've had healing, deliverance, all in those times when it has just been me on my own, seeking Him and humbling myself before Him. God has all this for us, and much more, if we would learn to bow down before Him, and set our hearts on Him. He is a God of restoration, and when we learn to walk in His ways, we will also walk in the reality of that restoration.

God is always looking for the best for us, but His best depends upon our surrender to His ways. A worshiper is someone who learns, like Paul did, to lay their lives down in order to seek his alone. The prize for the worshiper is not fame, money or power, but simply Jesus Himself, His like, His Joy, His peace, His restoration.

Proskuneo

One the main Greek words for worship is "Proskuneo."

The word "Proskuneo" literally means to move towards (*pros*) and to kiss (*kuneo.*) In the West we tend to think of kissing as being a romantic gesture, but it isn't the case here. The implication is not of romance, but of surrender to authority. In medieval times, when a man was made a lord by the king, that man would bow before the king, and kiss the back of his hand in reverence and surrender. This gesture, which is a common sign of surrender throughout mankind, and even in the animal kingdom, perfectly illustrates proskuneo worship.

One of my favourite biblical examples of true, proskuneo worship is from John 12: 1-8:

`"Six days before the Passover, Jesus came to Bethany, where Lazarus lived, whom Jesus had raised from the dead. Here a dinner was given in Jesus' honour. Martha served, while Lazarus was among those reclining at the table with him. Then Mary took about a pint of pure nard, an expensive perfume; she poured it on Jesus' feet and wiped his feet with her hair. And the house was filled with the fragrance of the perfume.

But one of his disciples, Judas Iscariot, who was later to betray him, objected, "Why wasn't this perfume sold and the money given to the poor? It was worth a year's wages. " He did not say this because he cared about the poor but because he was a thief; as keeper of the money bag, he used to help himself to what was put into it. "Leave her alone," Jesus replied. "It was intended that she should save this perfume for the day of my burial. You will always have the poor among you, but you will not always have me."

In this passage, we have two main characters: Mary and Judas. There is some debate over who exactly Mary of Bethany was, but whoever she was, she was someone of little importance. She had no worldly stature, and was a woman in a society that did not hold women in high regard. In essence, she was nothing, a woman who no one would notice or respect.

Contrast this with Judas. Judas was the most respectable of the apostles. He was in charge of the apostles' money, and probably had some kind of finance background. Judas was a man to be respected.

Mary's response to being close to Jesus is that of a true worshipper. She takes everything she has, (the perfume cost around one year's wages,) and she poured it out at Jesus' feet. She took all she owned, and laid it before Him, for no other reason than for Jesus' pleasure. She made herself the least, being content simply to be His presence.

Judas' reaction to Mary's outpouring was one of offence. Religion is always offended by genuine worship (see Michal despising David in 2 Samuel 6.) Judas' heart was not for Jesus, but to see his own glory. He talks about giving money to the poor, not out of love for the poor, but to make himself look good. Judas used religion as a vehicle to increase his own status.

These two people reacted differently to Jesus. One poured everything she had before Jesus, and the other was concerned only with increasing his own importance, in using Jesus to make himself more impressive to man.

The Heart

The difference between Mary and Judas is very simple; it is the difference of the heart. The difference in the state of the heart of these two followers of Jesus that determines how they responded to Jesus and how close they were to Him.

Our heart is where our desires come from. The desires of our heart is what drives us. Whatever we desire as a human is what leads us to take the actions we do. Our desires determine our decisions, the choices we make, our character and how we respond to those around us.

Originally, before the fall of man, man's heart was in perfect unison with God, and so man walked in unity with Him. When Adam and Eve rebelled against Him, though, sin entered man's heart, it no longer desired only God, but desired his own desires. Our hearts in their sinful state are about us, and rebellious towards God.

Each of us desires something for ourselves, be it attention, wealth, power, security, sex affection, to purchase something, stability or so on. The desires of each of us is different, and the extent to which we are driven by our hearts determines our character and behaviour. Just because we are Christians or in ministry, does not mean that our hearts are automatically correct. We can be in ministry, like Judas was, but use the name of Jesus to draw attention to ourselves, or to advance our own status, to look good and to impress men, or to develop our career within church organisation. This is very much something I have to battle with. My sinful state desires to draw attention to me, it craves to be the centre, rather than allowing Jesus to be the centre.

When I worship, I am actively deciding to surrender. I ask Jesus to change my heart and my focus, so that only He becomes the centre. I submit myself until I become unimportant, until only His desire and will counts. I lay down my own righteousness (ie the fact that I think I am right,) and accept His righteousness, (the fact that He is right.) As I worship, I ask Jesus to change my heart, so that it no longer desires its' own, but desires only what God Himself desires. Through the process of worship, our hearts are transformed from self focussed to God focussed.

As Jesus changes my heart in worship, I see and hear him more clearly. The result of my submission to Him is that I grow closer to him, I walk in greater unity with Him, I begin to desire what he desires. If I submitted perfectly to Him (which only the perfect person could ever do, ie Jesus,) then in theory I would walk as close to Him here on Earth as Adam did in the Garden of Eden.

"Who may ascend the mountain of the Lord? Who may stand in his holy place? The one who has clean hands and a pure heart, who does not trust in an idol or swear by a false god." (Psalm 24 3-4.)

The heart is the key to our encountering Jesus. It is only as our hearts are washed and purified by Him, through the process of worship, that we will draw near to Him. A pure heart is one that desires nothing for itself, but only desires Him and what He desires.

"You will seek me and find me when you seek me with all your heart." (Jeremiah 29:13.)

There is nothing as deceptive or corrupt as the human heart.

"The heart is deceitful above all things and beyond cure. Who can understand it?' (Jeremiah 17:9.)

Our hearts are most deceitful thing there is. As we generate a desire or point of view from our hearts, it is very hard for us to see past that desire being the correct one. We all assume that we are right, otherwise we wouldn't do what we are doing. We all think that our viewpoint as being right, and we measure other people by that, from the point of our own righteousness. If we are looking for a church, we generally have a set idea of what we would like from a church, what we want the music to be like, the preaching or the people or child care, and then we find somewhere that closest matches those desires. We judge other people according to the standards and viewpoints that we hold. We do this in every area of our lives. Our unchanged hearts are in a state of self righteousness, ie we are right, everything centres around what we think to be correct, and is judged by that standard. This sinful nature is how all our hearts are:

"All of us have become like one who is unclean, and all our righteous acts are like filthy rags..." (Isaiah 64:6)

The filthy rags referred to here in Isaiah are actually menstrual rags. That is the reality of our hearts outside of Jesus. Outside of Him, we are wrong. Jesus is the way and the truth, (John 14:6.) There is no truth outside of Him, nothing is right outside of Him. He is the very definition of truth. Nothing we generate out of ourselves is correct, and we are deception if we think it is.

When we worship, we actively lay down all that we think is right about ourselves, and we seek His righteousness. We have to realise the sinful nature of our hearts, and seek His heart, His desires. If we are not a people who live our lives in a state of worship , as Paul was, (Romans 12:1,) then we will walk in our own righteousness, in the desires of our own hearts, believing them to be correct. The only possible way to advance His Kingdom is if we have His heart. Without His heart, we will not see things as He does, which is the truth, but instead see things as we believe to be right, and in trying to do right, we will be deceived. In spite of our best intentions, and our believing our actions to be good, if we have not sought His heart, we will not walk in unity with Him, and not only will we not be advancing His kingdom, we will actively damage it.

We cannot judge right or wrong by our own hearts or perceptions. When Adam sinned, he ate from the tree of the knowledge of good and evil. His sin was to be able to discern right from wrong outside of God. There is no right outside of Jesus, there is no truth and there is nothing good outside of Him. If we do not spend our lives in a state of worship, we will miss His truth. Will we only find the truth in Him.

Each of us are called into different areas of ministry, some are called to be apostles, some pastors, some prophets, some evangelists, and some teachers (Ephesians 4:11.) There is a danger in taking on our calling, but without seeking His heart. The gifts of God are irrevocable (Romans 11:29,) they will not be taken away, but it is very easy to walk in those gifts in our own righteousness, acting as we believe to be right. Without seeking His heart in everything, the pastors will lead the people the wrong way, the teachers will teach incorrectly, the evangelists will evangelise out of their own strength and miss what God is doing. In short, the church will not function as it should, by Him working through us, but we will walk in our own ideas of what we should be doing. When we walk in our own righteousness, there will be no genuine power or Kingdom authority in anything we do. This is why seeking His heart must be the centre of all we do. When we do not seek Him, our churches will be full of us. Man's way is never the right way, *"There is a way that appears to be right, but in the end it leads to death." (Proverbs 14:12.)*

For God's bride, His church to become all that it is called to be, to function as it should function, we must give ourselves over to seeking His heart and His righteousness. We cannot see His church walk in that which it is called to without worship becoming the centre, as it is through worship that our hearts will be changed. We are called to minister to the world in unity with Him through His Spirit, but without submission to His heart and purposes, we will simply minister in our own flesh, which at best is useless, but at worst can actually damage the very people we want to minister to. Ministry that is generated out of our own unchanged hearts will not be true ministry at all, but will usually lead men to us, to what we are doing and to what we desire. Ministry that is in unity with His heart will always lead the people to Him, to his life, freedom and restoration.

"But seek first his kingdom and his righteousness, and all these things will be given to you as well." (Matthew 6:33.)

Broken

Judas' actions were no different from what goes on in most of us, (I very much include myself here.) Our natural instinct is to look good before men, especially those of us "on the platform" within our churches. Indeed, that is why many of us who are musicians became musicians, to look good in front of man. Our sinful state tries to take glory for ourselves, and tries to increase what we have, our importance, our sphere of influence, our ministry, our finances. Our hearts desire both man's affirmation and his admiration. Our hearts are no better than Judas', until God deals with them. That is why being broken by God is the most wonderful gift God can give us.

Being broken is when God breaks our own desires and our own will, so that we may turn our hearts to Him. We can only worship with a heart that is seeking Him for His own sake. When we use Jesus to lead men to ourselves, as Judas did, we are not worshiping, in spite of our religious appearance, but actually leading men to us rather than Him. We need to ask God to deal with our hearts, so that our only desire, like Mary, is to be happy being the least, just for the privilege of being close to Him. That is the pure heart that God desires in us. that is the heart that will walk with God.

This is a part of my story of being broken. I became a Christian when i was 17, after having a genuine encounter with God, and being a good musician in a small church, I quickly became part of the worship team. I am someone who likes to do things, I am a naturally driven person, I like to have purpose and ambition. Because this is my natural inclination, in the following weeks I quickly got involved in most things in the church, and subsequent churches I joined. I ran youth groups, music groups, outreaches, worship teams etc. in fact I did all those things that is encouraged in church. I was a "doer" I preached, I studied, I ministered. I went to all the meetings. I was busy with church, and church activity became my life. I got married, and was living in North Wales.

After around 10 years of this, God spoke to me. In fact, in all my years of church activity, I had never really heard His voice. I had "feelings" that I thought were him, but now He confronted me, via another person with these words, "you do not know me." Now, here was I, someone who had given many hundreds of hours to the church, to doing what I assumed was His work, being told by God that I did not know Him. i did not believe what God was saying, and my pride struggled to accept what God was saying. How dare someone say that I did not know God? Could they not see who I was? I rallied against the word of God for some days, maybe even weeks. The person who brought me the message must be wrong; the problem lies with them, not me. And yet even in my state of self-righteousness, and anger, I knew it was God who sent me the message. At that point I had a choice. Either continue as I was, or repent. There was a small part of me that knew I had to repent, and accept that I had no real relationship with God, that I was caught up in the treadmill of church activity without really knowing Him. I got on my bed, and decided that I was going to seek God until I found Him.

I started confessing my sin, confessing that I had no desire for God. As I started seeking, praying and confessing, I started to get a true taste of His glory. The more I repented and prayed, the closer I got. After about 3 hours of this the Heavens began to open, and I began to see God in His glory. The repentance became liberating, exhilarating, leading me closer to Him. He began to show me truth of my Christian life so far, that it was built entirely on my own strength, on my own righteousness, my own pride and ambition. At best, my "ministry" up to that point had been useless, at worst dangerous and damaging. I knew, sitting in His presence that this is what I really wanted, that this is what the reality of a Christian walk should be. I phoned my pastor and resigned from all church activities. The thought of leading worship again made me feel physically sick, knowing how I had been doing it without God. I resolved that I would never do anything within church again, until He commanded me otherwise. My place from then on was going to be spent like Mary of Bethany, at the feet of Jesus, enjoying Him alone.

The following weeks were an absolute joy. I spent as much time as I could just seeking God. Reading the Bible, which I had always found quite dull, suddenly came to life, every verse I read, though I had read them many times before, were full of revelation. I could not get enough of His word, or of seeking Him. I had been saved 10 years before, and had been filled with the Holy Spirit, and had the occasional encounter with God, usually when someone else prayed with me, and was sometimes around the genuine things of God, but from the point of being saved I never really developed my own relationship with God. What I had thought of as walking with God was actually just church activity, of which I did plenty. I gave lip service to God, I said the right things, acted (outwardly,) the right way, and yet I did not KNOW Him. I knew all about Him, yet had no actual relationship with Him. In my doing, I had missed the whole point, and the point is Him.

In the years since then, I have been totally transformed as a person, both physically and in terms of character. By walking in submission to Him, He has been able to work on me, changing me, teaching me, maturing me. that work is ongoing, and I am well aware how my heart needs continue to change, but I also know that I am a witness to how He transforms. the redemptive, restoring work of Jesus is a reality. Religion talks about Him, but a genuine walk with Him sees real transformation. Religion, empty words, (even charismatic religion,) never changed anything, but the reality of Jesus does.

The key to true worship is brokenness and repentance. We have to repent of anything that comes between us and His will, which is so much more than the "bad things" which we know we ought not to do. It is everything that resists the Spirit of God, everything we try to build ourselves, our families, our churches, our businesses, we have to give them back to Him and allow His Spirit to operate in them. We must take up the highest place of all, the place of a servant, having no will, no desire but Jesus Himself. That is the worship that God has for our lives and our churches. That is the proskuneo worship that God desires in His church.

On the Sermon on the Mount, Jesus proclaimed, Matthew 5:3 "*Blessed are the poor in spirit, for theirs is the kingdom of heaven.*"Jesus did not say, "blessed are the poor," as is often misquoted, but "blessed are the poor in spirit." Our spirit determines our will, our desire. The poor in spirit are the broken or the humble, those who have no will apart from what Jesus desires. Jesus said that it is a blessing to be broken, because then, we will walk in the Kingdom of Heaven.

If our lives and churches are to see the true power and restoration work of Jesus, then we must begin to deal with our hearts as individuals. It is only through our decision to worship, to surrender ourselves and seek Him, that our hearts can be changed, and we can walk in unity with Jesus. Ministry that comes out of our own strength and ability is not ministry, it may make us look and feel good, but it is not His work, it is ours. it will lead men only to us and what we are establishing. When our churches are broken to Jesus' will, to seeking Him, to serving Him, then we will be a people who truly walk in Kingdom authority and power. Only then will we be a people who can change our families, or towns or even nations. This is our calling, but to achieve our calling, we must allow our hearts to be turned to Him alone. It is only through true worship that our hearts can be transformed.

If My People..

In the Old testament, God illustrates His character through His relationship with His people, the Israelites. There are times when they walked in faithfulness to God and His commands, and these times resulted in success and blessings. There are other times when they rebelled against God, they complained about Him, walked away from Him, built their own idols, and forgot about Him.

The Israelite's tendency to walk in their own ways, despite all that God did with them, is the same tendency that we have today. Their hearts then were the same as ours today. Having experienced many different cultures around the world, one thing I have learned is that man's heart is the same no matter what the culture or background.

Because man's heart naturally seeks its' own, God taught His people, first through the tabernacles of Moses and David, (which we will look at later,) and then later through the Temple, that He was to be the centre of their nation. His Presence was established amongst them, and the Israelites were instructed to continually return to Him in worship and sacrifice, that they would not wander off in their own ways, but remain loyal to His ways. His people were called to keep themselves separate and Holy to Him wherever they were, whether they were wandering the wilderness, or established in great cities. His Presence, and the requirement of obedience by the Children of Israel, was placed at the centre of all that they did.

'But you are a chosen people, a royal priesthood, a holy nation, God's special possession, that you may declare the praises of him who called you out of darkness into his wonderful light.' (1 Peter 2:9.)

The people of God are called to be that holy nation. The word "church" comes from the Greek word "Ekklesia." This word literally means to be "called out." Our calling is to be separate from the land that we live in. We are called to live in the world, but not to operate as the world does. We are called to holiness, ie to be set apart, distinct.

"Do not conform to the pattern of this world..." (Romans 12:2)

The world has its' own way of operation. It works by power, manipulation, self seeking, self promotion, money, alliances and covenants. In short, it operates in the flesh. The world always seeks it own, and seeks to achieve its own through fleshly means, through whatever method it can employ. It tries to advance itself, to get what it can, to get what it desires, to seek its' own fulfilment and its' own happiness. The world always acts according to what it perceives will be best for it, a vision that is skewed without looking at God.

That is fine for the world. The world will act as the world acts, but that is not our calling. Our calling is to be a people not who work through the flesh, but through the Spirit. John the Baptist, Jesus and later the apostles all carried the same message, "Repent, for the kingdom of heaven is at hand." This message was to His people, telling them to no longer act as the world acts, because the Kingdom of God is here. Because Jesus has paid the price for our sins, we have full access to the Father and all that is His. We do not need to carry on as the world does, we do not need to build as they do. A person of God does not try to advance their cause, even their Christian cause, through fleshly means, but rather operates in Jesus through the Spirit. A person of God operates direct through Jesus, not through their own ability. They take the lowest place, knowing that if Jesus wants to promote them, He can. They take the place of the servant, of the lowly. When our hearts have been transformed, we will no longer desire what the world desires, and so we will not act like it does. Above all, as children of God, we are called to keep our hearts pure, that they desire nothing but what God desires, not caring about the world and what it desires, but only looking to Jesus and His heart.

The Temple

God understands our hearts soon become corrupted or tempted by the things of this world, leading us to act like the world, which is why He established His Temple in the centre of His nation, as a place where the Israelites could worship Him and turn their hearts to Him.

When Solomon dedicated the first Temple, God appeared to him, and gave him this message:

"If my people, who are called by my name, will humble themselves and pray and seek my face and turn from their wicked ways, then I will hear from heaven, and I will forgive their sin and will heal their land." (2 Chronicles 7:14.)

The Temple of God was given to the Israelites for four functions: for the people to humble themselves, to pray, to seek His face and to turn from wicked ways.

The first word of this verse is "*if*." The promises of God are conditional. When we do our part, God promises to do His. If we are not prepared to do what God says, then he will not do His. God tells us the condition upon which He will heal our land, and it is dependent upon our submission to Him, not upon if we can establish a dynamic ministry, or preach well, or reach more followers with our social network, but only *if* we will humble ourselves, pray, seek His face and repent. God always requires our obedience before He moves.

The calling is upon God's people who are called by His name, ie the *ekklesia*, the church, to humble ourselves. This was the function of the Temple, that we would lay ourselves down, or in other words, worship Him. When we lay ourselves down, we rely not upon ourselves but upon Him, we turn ourselves to His ways.

Pray

Prayer is the ultimate expression of humility. When we turn to prayer, we are humbling ourselves and acknowledging our reliance upon Jesus. Prayer is about relying on the Spirit over our own flesh. When we pray, we are surrendering our flesh, laying it down, and instead turning to Him. Prayer is the manifestation of our reliance upon God alone. A person who turns to prayer, rather than reacts in the flesh out of their own righteousness, is one who abides in Jesus.

In Matthew 6, Jesus teaches us how to pray:

"This, then, is how you should pray: Our Father in heaven ,hallowed be your name, your kingdom come, your will be done, on earth as it is in heaven. Give us today our daily bread. And forgive us our debts, as we also have forgiven our debtors. And lead us not into temptation, but deliver us from the evil one."

There is such a strong correlation between prayer and worship, and it is sometimes hard to distinguish where one begins and the other ends.. The Greek word for prayer is *proseuchomai*, which is very similar to the word *proskuneo* for worship. Proseuchomai means to turn our desires to God. It is the reliance upon Him for everything. The Lord's prayer begins with: "Our Father in heaven, hallowed be your name, your kingdom come, your will be done, on earth as it is in heaven…" These words are worship in action. They are focussing on Jesus, acknowledging His authority, seeking His Kingdom, and setting our hearts in line with Him, so that we desire His Kingdom, not ours. From that place of seeking His will, any need we have we look to Him for. True prayer is all about reliance upon Him.

We also forgive others as we pray, which is again a part of our acceptance that we have no righteousness of our own, and that we are as guilty as anyone else. We forgive, because we know that our hearts are just as bad, and He has forgiven us. We do not forgive from a place of self righteousness, of assuming that we are in the right but we will forgive anyway, rather we forgive out of accepting that we have no more righteousness than anyone else, we need Jesus' forgiveness as much as anyone. As we forgive others from that place of humility, so we can be forgiven.

The temple was established as a place of prayer, a place of reliance upon Him, of trusting in Him.

We may also fast alongside our praying. Fasting, like prayer, is another expression of humility, or reliance upon Him. Fasting is representative of our surrendering our own bodies, our flesh, and looking just to His Spirit. The power of fasting is often overlooked in our western society.

Jesus said "My house will be called a house of prayer,...." (Matthew 21:13.) That is how His house was called to be when He established the Temple, and it is what it is called to be now. Our own lives and our churches should be a place of seeking Him and reliance upon Him, a place not of man's works, but of God's.

Seek His Face

Interlinked with prayer and worship, we are called to "seek His face." Note it is His face we are called to seek. Seeking His face means to seek His character, to seek His personality, or in other words, to know Him. I know my wife's face. I can discern what she is thinking at any one point in time, because I know her face. If she is unhappy, it is impossible for her to hide it, because I know her face. She may fool other people, but not me, because I know her. We are told to seek Jesus' face in the same way. When we walk in intimacy with Him, we begin to get in tune with His heart, we begin to see things how He sees them, to love what He loves, to hate what He hates. This level of intimacy cannot be taught, but can only be gained through spending time seeking Him and His thoughts. It is about knowing Him, rather than just knowing about Him. We are called not just to seek His hand (ie His works,) but His character, His heart too.

Repenting

Lastly, God instructed His temple to be a place where we turn from our wicked ways, or in other words, repent. As I mentioned earlier, repentance is such a strong message throughout the Old Testament and the New, it was central to the message of the prophets, apostles and even Jesus himself. It is also a part of how Jesus taught us to pray, and a part of worship. Turning from our own ways, our ways of the flesh, and instead following His ways is a cornerstone of His Temple.

This is what God's house has always been intended to be, a place of seeking, repenting, praying and humbling ourselves. Every great revival that has ever happened have not been moves of church activity, but moves of repentance, humbling, praying and seeking.

The house of God is a place where Jesus is put in the centre, not just talking about Him, but each of us encountering Him, seeking Him, desiring Him. The house of God is not a place where we come to hear second hand information about God, or to do activity around God, but a place where we encounter Him personally. Every activity of our meeting, be it the worship or the word, or anything else should be geared towards leading the people to Jesus Himself.

God promises than when we give our lives, churches, house groups or meetings over to these works, then He will heal our land, as we have seen with many mighty moves of God in the past, and as I can personally testify in so many areas of my own life. In John 6, Jesus is asked about what work they should be doing. Jesus replies that our work is to "believe in the one he has sent..." (John 6:29.) Our work is to trust in Him, look to him, live in Him, rather than to go off on our own and attempt to accomplish His works our own ways. When we are broken and surrendered to Him, we will walk with Him, and impact the world more than any of our activity outside of Him could ever achieve.

In the Old testament, the people were given a physical temple or tabernacle, which housed the Presence of God in the centre, for the people to worship.

'Do you not know that your bodies are temples of the Holy Spirit, who is in you, whom you have received from God? You are not your own.' 1 Corinthians 6:19

When the Holy Spirit enters us, we ourselves become The temple of God. His Spirit lives not in a box in a building, but in us. That does not mean, however that we forget all that God showed His people in the Old Testament. Jesus did not come to abolish the law, but to fulfil it, (Matthew 5:17.) God has revealed His heart to us through the Old Testament, and he still desires that we use our temples, our lives, to humble ourselves, pray, seek His face and repent. His Temple in Israel was precious and meticulously made. It was perfect in all ways, because it housed Him. That too is our calling, to be temples that honour Him in every area, in obedience, love and faithfulness. It is through these temples that God will minister to the world and His people.

When the church met together in the New testament, it was also to pray, to worship and to prophesy. Our meetings, whether they be in the grandest cathedral or the lowliest house, should be places where we seek him, submit to Him and worship Him. In short, they should be places of *encounter.* His promise is still valid today: *If* we humble ourselves, seek His face, pray and repent, *then* He will heal our land. Without Him, our meetings are just religious exercises, when we seek Him, our lives will manifest His glory and power.

The Levites

All religious activity in the Old testament had one purpose, to lead people to God. The role of leading the people there was so important, that it was not given to just anyone. God could only trust one of the tribes of Israel with this task, the Levites. The Levites were a people set aside, from amongst God's people, with the job of ministering to Him and leading the Israelites into God's presence. They were given the priestly role, because their hearts were different than the other tribes.

In Exodus 32, after the Israelites had been set free from slavery in Egypt, Moses went up to Mount Sinai, where he received the 10 commandments. With the Israelites left without their leader, their shepherd, they soon began to forget all that God had done for them, and in their impatience, ill-discipline and rebellion, began to take matters into their own hands.

"When the people saw that Moses was so long in coming down from the mountain, they gathered around Aaron and said, "Come, make us gods who will go before us. As for this fellow Moses who brought us up out of Egypt, we don't know what has happened to him." Aaron answered them, "Take off the gold earrings that your wives, your sons and your daughters are wearing, and bring them to me." So all the people took off their earrings and brought them to Aaron. He took what they handed him and made it into an idol cast in the shape of a calf, fashioning it with a tool. Then they said, "These are your gods, Israel, who brought you up out of Egypt." When Aaron saw this, he built an altar in front of the calf and announced, "Tomorrow there will be a festival to the Lord." So the next day the people rose early and sacrificed burnt offerings and presented fellowship offerings. Afterward they sat down to eat and drink and got up to indulge in revelry."(Exodus 32:1-10.)

It is amazing how quickly the people forget how God had redeemed them. Rather than having the patience to wait upon God, on what he was doing with them, it was far easier to create their own god out of their own resources. Moses was only gone 40 days, yet without their shepherd, the character and hearts of the people were exposed, and they soon gave up on waiting on God, and built their own religion.

The heart of a servant is a faithful one. A servant does not move unless asked. A servant waits for the command of their master. The Israelites at this point did not have a servants heart. They were happy to get the good things from God, the freedom, the miracles, the provision, and yet when faithfulness was required, they were not found waiting, but doing their own works, just like the foolish virgins in Matthew 25.

It is interesting that with their wealth they choose to build a god. They wanted religion, yet they wanted it to be on their terms, out of their own strength. They moulded God in to the image that they thought he should be, how they found acceptable. they wanted God on demand, rather than humbling themselves, seeking Him and being faithful. It is so much easier to create out of our own ability or resources, rather than to be faithful and wait.

Jesus' inheritance is often called "the bride," in the Bible. (Rev 19:7, Rev 21:2, John 3:29, etc..)

"For I feel a divine jealousy for you, since I betrothed you to one husband, to present you as a pure virgin to Christ." (2 Cor 11:2.)

A bride is faithful. A bride is a virgin. She offers herself to no man, rather she keeps herself pure for her husband. That is what His church is called to be, a pure, unblemished bride, who only has eyes for her husband, who remains faithful only to Him. The Israelites here, like us so often, were not prepared to wait for their husband. Rather than keep themselves pure, they became unfaithful, because in spite of everything He had done for them, they ultimately wanted their own satisfaction. They had not the patience, the character or the desire to wait upon God for what he was doing, it was far easier to "sleep around," to get their wants satisfied elsewhere.

When Moses came down from the mountain, his anger burned against them. He realised that the Israelites, God's chosen and holy ones had become a laughing stock to their enemies (vs 25.) So it is when we create religion out of our own hands because of our unfaithfulness. Our enemy's do not respect those called to be a holy nation, who have turned against faithfulness to the true God, and instead worship gods of their own making, which hold no power. The enemy recognises when we follow the real God and walk in His authority, and when we have just empty religion. Empty religion is mocked by the world. The world sees it for what it is, powerless. When our churches create powerless works out of our own hands, the world recognises it. We may build out of our own hands, but what we build carries no real authority. It is for this reason the Israelites were laughed at by their enemies, and it is the same reason the church today carries so little respect in our society. *"As it is written: "God's name is blasphemed among the Gentiles because of you."* (Romans 2:24.) We are God's representatives. The world knows Him through His people. When His people operate in the same way that the world operates, we dishonour Him and bring mockery to His name.

"So he stood at the entrance to the camp and said, *"Whoever is for the Lord, come to me." And all the Levites rallied to him," (Exodus 32:26.)*

When Moses saw what had gone on in his absence, he declared, "*who is on the side of the Lord?*" It was a question for God's people, for His church - who is on God's side? God was not asking the world who wanted to follow Him, but His church, his chosen people. Out of all those called by His name, who was willing to lay down their own agenda, and to seek His? Who was willing to humble themselves, lay down their lives of follow Him?

When this challenge went out, only one of the twelve tribes of Israel stepped forward, the Levites. The Levites demonstrated that out of all God's people, they were willing to to follow God. Jesus carried the same message. Many people declared that they wanted to follow Jesus, and He would challenge each of them to take up their cross, to leave their family or to leave their wealth. To truly follow Jesus, we have to lay ourselves down, we have to give up what we think is right, and seek what He is doing. This the heart that the Levites had. This is the heart of a worshiper. It was because of their heart that the Levites were entrusted with taking the people into His presence. Aaron and his line were called into the priesthood, (Aaron was a Levite,) and those Levites who were not priests were given other forms of service before God. (See numbers 3:12-13, Deuteronomy 10:8 and Numbers 8:19.)

Then Moses said, *"You have been set apart to the Lord today, for you were against your own sons and brothers, and he has blessed you this day." (Exodus 32:29.)*

The Levites were set aside for God's purposes. They did not inherit land like the rest of the Israelites - God himself was to be their inheritance. They were not to be concerned with the cares of this world, but with the things of God.

The Levites are a biblical example to those called to lead worship today. When God appointed the Levites, he did not look for those with the most musical talent, or for the best public speakers, or for the most charismatic or even for the most educated tribe. He called the tribe whose hearts desired Him. That is the only qualification God looks for in His people. There is a saying that states that God does not call the qualified, he qualifies the called. When God has a person whose heart is after Him, He can train, refine and disciple them to mould them into the person they need to be to fulfill their calling. That all takes time, as God matures us and shapes our character. A heart that desires Him is willing to be changed and refined His way, and so will be brought to true maturity.

David

David was such a man. When God was looking to raise up a king for His nation, He found David. David was the youngest of eight brothers, the least important one. He was a shepherd, a person who spent his life doing a relatively lowly job. His brother was more physically impressive than him, and would have made an ideal choice of king if left to the desires of the people or Samuel, but God rejected David's brother Eliab.

"Do not consider his appearance or his height, for I have rejected him. The LORD does not look at the things people look at. People look at the outward appearance, but the LORD looks at the heart." (1 Samuel 16:7)

There were many more qualified people than David to run a nation, and in fact, David was probably the least likely of all the people to be chosen. However, God saw David's heart, not his strength, intellect or charisma. God knew that in David, he had a man who would seek His own heart.

"After removing Saul, he made David their king. God testified concerning him: 'I have found David son of Jesse, a man after my own heart; he will do everything I want him to do." (Acts 13:22.)

That is still the only qualification to being a servant of God, of serving in His house, of leading men into His presence. A person who's heart desires God can be trained, refined, disciplined and matured. A person who's heart seeks God will be willing to go through being discipled. They will be humble enough to accept correction, or even endure hardship, just for the prize of knowing Him.

David was by no means a perfect man. He had an adulterous affair and effectively murdered someone to satisfy his own fleshly desire. However, what made him different was that in spite of the times he gave into the flesh or made mistakes, he returned to God with humility, with genuine repentance. He messed up, but always came back to putting God first, because His heart was a heart that was after God's heart.

Those who God calls are rarely perfect. Most of the people in the Bible have flawed characters, and many of our Biblical examples are murderers, liars or thieves when God calls them. What makes them different, though, is that they had hearts that were willing to lose everything just to be obedient to God, just to follow Him. Many people are have callings on their lives but only a few are willing to do things God's way to the point where they fulfil those callings. The way of the flesh puffs us up, makes us important, leads us to creating with our own resources, to make ourselves into a success. The way of the Spirit is a way of sacrifice and surrender, in order to follow Him. His way is a way that changed our character, that we would be able to walk in what God has for us. This is the heart God looks for.

For many are called, but few are chosen. (Matthew 22:14.)

We sometimes too easily judge people on the things of the flesh that impress us, be that worldly qualifications, charisma, skills or so on. these Things are obviously not wrong in themselves, and are even desirable, but they are not the qualification that God looks for in His house. When we fill our leadership positions simply with those with desirable fleshly qualities, our churches will be dominated by those characteristics. His House is a house of seeking, prayer, repentance and humility. If our churches are led by people who have hearts like David, who desired God's heart, then our meetings will become places that are given over to chasing God's heart.

The Kingdom of God belongs the poor of spirit, to the pure hearted, to those who make peace, to the meek, to those who hunger and thirst for righteousness, to the merciful and to those who are persecuted for the sake of His righteousness.

"But God chose the foolish things of the world, that he might put to shame them that are wise; and God chose the weak things of the world, that he might put to shame the things that are strong." (1 Corinthians 27.)

True spiritual fathers are essential in this time. If we fill our churches with those whose hearts are not after God, but are qualified in a worldly sense, then those whose hearts do desire God, but are perhaps unskilled, unrefined, or their characters do not fit, will remain unnurtured. We need spiritual fathers who will stand with those whose hearts are right, but maybe immature or untrained, to see them become the person they are called to be. We need both fathers, and true children, those who are willing to be changed and disciplined, not because they desire professional ministry, but God.

I have been so caught up in church activity, or "ministry," as I believed it was, that everything became about the activity, rather than leading people directly to God. This is because as I moved through church, my heart was not correct. I recognise this now, but did not realise it at the time. In turn what i produced was not people after God's heart, but more church activity. Nobody ever got changed in themselves, it was merely ministry for the sake of ministry, (although it was not really ministry at all.) A true shepherd leads the people to The Shepherd, to Jesus himself, just like the Levites did. This should be the focus of all our churches and households, to seek Him, to humble ourselves, to pray and to repent. Only hearts that desire God desire these activities. It is too easy to establish our own works out of our own resources, like most of Israel did. The true ministers, like the Levites, are the ones who lay themselves aside in order to be on the side of the Lord.

Entering God's presence - The Tabernacle of Moses

God's setting free of the Israelites is symbolic of His setting us free from slavery. One of the first things God does with the Israelites after setting them free, is reveal His desire for His people to be close to Him.

In Exodus 25:22, God Instructs the Israelites to construct a tabernacle where *"I will meet with you."* The word "Tabernacle" comes from the Hebrew word, "*mishkan*," meaning "place of dwelling" or the resting place for the presence of God. The tabernacle was a tent, in the centre of which was housed the very presence of God. It was a place established specifically so that His people could draw near to Him.

"Now the first covenant had regulations for worship and also an earthly sanctuary. A tabernacle was set up. In its first room were the lampstand, the table and the consecrated bread; this was called the Holy Place. Behind the second curtain was a room called the Most Holy Place, which had the golden altar of incense and the gold-covered ark of the covenant. This ark contained the gold jar of manna, Aaron's staff that had budded, and the stone tablets of the covenant. Above the ark were the cherubim of the Glory, overshadowing the atonement cover. But we cannot discuss these things in detail now. When everything had been arranged like this, the priests entered regularly into the outer room to carry on their ministry. But only the high priest entered the inner room, and that only once a year, and never without blood, which he offered for himself and for the sins the people had committed in ignorance. The Holy Spirit was showing by this that the way into the Most Holy Place had not yet been disclosed as long as the first tabernacle was still standing. This is an illustration for the present time, indicating that the gifts and sacrifices being offered were not able to clear the conscience of the worshiper. They are only a matter of food and drink and various ceremonial washings external regulations applying until the time of the new order." (Hebrews 9: 1-11.)

Verse 8 – 9 tells us that the Tabernacle was a symbol, or representation of how to enter into the Holiest of Holies. It was built to show us today how to enter into the presence of God. God had to show His people that you cannot enter into the presence of the Holy one any way we want to, we have to enter on His terms, how He demands.

The way in which God taught the Israelites to enter into His presence is a through a journey of sacrifice. In the Old Testament, God taught a system of ceremonial sacrifice that led to His presence, which has been fulfilled by Jesus becoming our sacrifice. However, Although Jesus has become our literal sacrifice, paying the price for our sins, it does not mean that we do not sacrifice at all. To follow Jesus still requires a sacrifice, not a physical one, but a sacrifice of our lives, our desire, our hearts and our will. Jesus said, *"Whoever wants to be my disciple must deny themselves and take up their cross daily and follow me." Luke 9:23.* To be close to Him, we must deny ourselves. The journey into Gods' presence is still a journey of sacrifice, but not a dead religious sacrifice, but the sacrifice of a surrendered life.

"You do not delight in sacrifice, or I would bring it; you do not take pleasure in burnt offerings. The sacrifices of God are a broken spirit; a broken and contrite heart, O God, you will not despise." Psalm 51 16-1

The Tabernacle of Moses

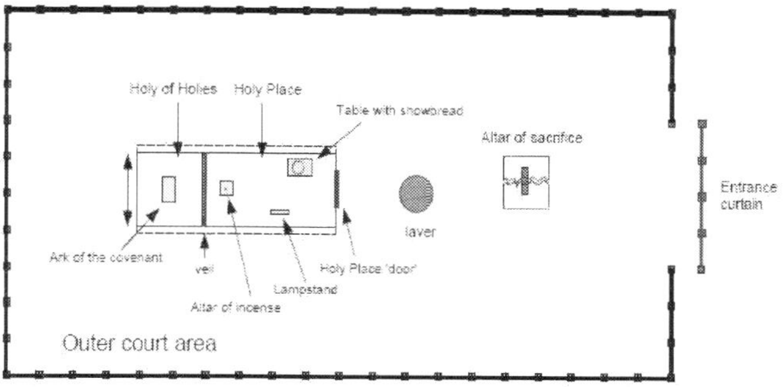

The above diagram shows the layout of the Tabernacle of Moses.

There are 3 areas of the tabernacle, the Outer Court Area, the Holy Place and the Holy of Holies. The Israelites entered into the tabernacle from the east. God gave them a system to enter into the Holy of Holies (where only the high priest could go.)

Entering His courts – praise vs. worship

"Enter his gates with thanksgiving, and his courts with praise; give thanks to him and praise his name." (Psalm 100:4.)

As the Israelites entered His courts, they were instructed to do so with praise. Is praise the same thing as worship? No. We have seen how the Greek word for worship is *proskunueo*, (the Hebrew equivalent is *shachah*,) which we have seen means to submit to God, to bow down, to surrender. Yet God is giving a specific command to enter with *praise,* as opposed to worship.

So what is praise? There are many different words for praise in the Bible, but most have a similar meaning. In this verse, the words being used here are *towadah* and *tehillah.*

The word *towdah* means to give thanks. It is thanking God for what he has done, and for what He will do. The power of praise is a powerful thing. It is the proclamation of what God has done, what He has achieved. It is agreement with the truth. Today, we can thank God for all Jesus has done for us. When we are oppressed or discouraged, we speak out the truth of what God has done. If we are ill, we proclaim His healing.

In Ephesians 6, Paul talks about the word of God being our sword. This is a practical application of this. As we proclaim God's truth – as opposed to what we may feel, or see in the physical, strongholds shake, and chains are broken. This is how God told the Israelites to enter in, with the attitude of truth and thanksgiving.

Tehillah means to sing, to laud. Again it is a proclaiming word. All the words for praise are noisy, boastful, and celebratory. They are based on truth. True praise is spiritual warfare. A church that knows who it is, and does not look to itself and its' own problems are a mighty army. When Jehoshaphat went into battle in 2 Chronicles 20, he understood this truth. He sent the musicians first, with towdah, thanksgiving praise, which led them to victory.

So our first step in entering the presence of God is thanksgiving and praise – proclaiming the truth of who Jesus is and what He has done. Praise and worship are separate, but both important. The goal is entering His presence. The first part of that journey is praise. Some of the Hebrew words for praise are physical, they involve raising hands or creating loud noise. As we obey God by praising, we are submitting our body to Him. As we use our body to proclaim truth, it submits to what God says, over whatever we may feel.

"Through Jesus, therefore, let us continually offer to God a sacrifice of praise--the fruit of lips that confess his name." (Hebrews 13:15.)

Praise, therefore, is our first sacrifice in entering His presence. It is acting on truth however we feel, it is surrendering our body to what He says, not to how what we want.

Worship, and worship leading, is a journey, it is a journey into the Presence of God. If we are leading worship, we have to keep this in mind. True praise is a powerful thing, but it is only the beginning of our journey. A lot of churches love to praise, which is great, but we must remember to keep moving forward if we are to enter into a deeper place with God. Praise only gets us past His gates. It is also important to keep in mind the journey if you are using songs. Identify which songs that you use are worship, and which are praise, and use the praise songs first, flowing into the worship songs. It is important not to keep changing between praise and worship. The Levites led the people into the presence of God, and we must do the same.

Going deeper

Praise was our first sacrifice, if we are to go deeper, we must continue to sacrifice ourselves.

The first item the Israelites encountered on their journey through the tabernacle was the alter of sacrifice. The Israelites has to bring an unblemished animal to the priest for sacrifice, on behalf of the sin of the person. God was showing the people how sin needs to be paid for in blood. Today, as we worship, our next step to drawing closer to God is acknowledging and confessing our sin before God, and accepting the blood of Jesus as the price for our sin. This is why one of Jesus' many titles is a lamb. He is our sacrifice.

Next was the laver, or wash basin, which was a bronze bowl of water. This is where the priests washed their hands and feet, before drawing closer to God in the Holy place. Again, the washing is symbolic of Jesus washing away our sins.

We started entering God's presence by praise – acknowledging the truth of Jesus, and proclaiming it. We draw into the Holy Place by repentance, acknowledging our weaknesses, and accepting Jesus' sacrifice for our sins.

The priests could then enter the Holy Place. The first item in the Holy place was the lamp stand, or menorah. A menorah has 7 candles, a central candle with 6 smaller candles by its' side. The priests were instructed to never let the candles go out. A menorah is another prophetic of the characteristics of Jesus. Jesus is the light of the world, (John 8:12, John 12:46,) and we too are to represent that light, (Mathew 5:14) Light represents truth. We are called to worship God is Spirit and truth, (John 4:20-24.) The truth of Jesus is an important part of worship.

There was also a table of bread in the Holy Place, where fresh bread was placed. The bread signifies the human will. To make bread, the wheat is ground into flour, as our will must be. Next, it is put through fire, as our wills must be tested and purified by fire. Our will must be submitted to God. This is the process of being broken, as I have discussed previously.

Lastly, in the Holy Place was an alter of incense, where the priests burned incense. Incense is prophetic of prayer from the saints, rising up to God (see Psalm 141:2, Revelations 8 3-4.) Prayer and worship are closely related, and as the prayers of God's children go up to God, it is like incense filling God's nostrils. True prayer comes out of worship, it is our being broken before God, and as we are broken and weak in ourselves, we then have to rely on God to move. You cannot have true prayer without worship, without surrender. The prayer that moves God is prayer that comes out of that place of brokenness. When Jesus taught us to pray (Matthew 6:13-19) it starts off we surrendering before God, focusing our hearts and our minds upon Jesus, and acknowledging His lordship, all of which is simply worship, before then petitioning God for our needs out of that place of brokenness and surrender. God calls His house a" house of prayer for all nations,"(Isaiah 56:3) This is how HE sees His house, a place where, out of our brokenness, our prayers continually go up before God. There are ministries around the globe where there is continual prayer, continual incense into God's presence. This is what God has ordained His house to be.

So truth, brokenness and prayer led the priest into the Presence of God, into the Most Holy Place. The most Holy Place or Holy of Holies literally housed the presence of God, in the Ark of the Covenant. A veil, or curtain separated the Most Holy Place. God kept His presence separate, and only the high priest could enter this place and survive.

"But only the high priest entered the inner room, and that only once a year, and never without blood, which he offered for himself and for the sins the people had committed in ignorance." (Hebrews 9:7)

So the Presence of God was closed to man. When Jesus dies, this veil of separation was torn in two (Matthew 27:51.) Jesus' blood sacrifice meant that the price of our sinfulness had been paid in full. We are now free to enter into the Most Holy Place, through Jesus, our High Priest. Through this process of brokenness and surrender, we can end up in the very throne room of God. Too many of us choose to live our lives on the outskirts of Gods' presence, never entering into His fullness. But a true worshiper will sacrifice their life for the sake of drawing near to God. I have had a few times in my life where I literally could not stand – the weight of God's glory has been too heavy. This has always happened after periods of prolonged seeking and surrendering. It is the most awesome thing, the power of which is completely indescribable, but I'm sure that even then I have been just getting a tiny glimpse of who Jesus is.

The veil has been torn, though Jesus our High Priest. God has made a way for us to be close to Him, as it was in the Garden of Eden, but in this age we still have free will. We can choose sin and self at any time, or we can choose selflessness and God's purpose. The more we choose God in our lives, our minds, our hearts, the closer we draw near. We are always as close to God as we want to be.

These are the terms on which God requires us to enter into His presence. As we revere God, we go to Him on His terms, in faithfulness to Him, rather than how we find acceptable. True sacrifice is the sacrifice that God requires, not what we are prepared to give, but what He demands.

Picking up our cross

"Then Jesus said to his disciples, "Whoever wants to be my disciple must deny themselves and take up their cross and follow me." (Matthew 16:24.)

Jesus taught so many basic truths about what is to know Him and follow Him, truths that we as His people need to return to again and again. Man's heart being what it is, tries to twist the things of God to make it all about us. Somehow, we have ended up making our walk with God being all about us, us being catered to, to us being kept happy, to us getting what we want on our terms. When we make our churches all about man's will and desires, we loose the absolute basics about what it is to be a Christian, and our churches become places with no power or life, because we are focussed upon man rather than God.

There are a few accounts in the Bible of people desiring to follow Jesus, and He gave each of them a condition to following Him. To one man, Jesus challenged him to leave all his wealth, in order to follow Him (Luke 18:22.) To another, Jesus told him to leave burying his father (Luke 9:60,) and to another to not even say goodbye to his family (Luke 9:62.) To the following crowds, Jesus said this:

"Large crowds were travelling with Jesus, and turning to them he said: "If anyone comes to me and does not hate father and mother, wife and children, brothers and sisters—yes, even their own life—such a person cannot be my disciple. And whoever does not carry their cross and follow me cannot be my disciple." (Luke 14:25-27.)

Jesus made it clear, if we are to follow Him, then we follow Him on His terms. We cannot expect Him to get involved in what we are doing on our terms. This is a distortion of what it is to be a true follower of Christ. When Jesus told us to pick up our cross and follow Him, it means simply that we are to sacrifice ourselves, to lay down our own lives, to give ourselves over to doing things His way, not to trying to get Jesus involved on what we are doing on His behalf.

True worship is an understanding of this truth, that we are the tail, not the head, the followers not the leader, the least, not the highest. Again, the apostle Paul walked in this revelation, and as a result, God was able to use him to build His church more than anybody else in history. That is the power of a broken life, one dedicated to seeking and following Him.

Because we in the church understand the power of Jesus' sacrifice on the cross, that He took our sins and paid the price, and that our salvation does not come from works, we have sometimes misunderstood that to mean that there is no cost to following Jesus. It is absolutely true that He paid once and for all for our sins, and that we cannot earn salvation through our works or effort. Salvation is there for anybody who calls on His name (Romans 10:13,) but to truly be his disciple, His follower, carries a cost. The cost is our lives. Everything that we desire in our hearts has to be sacrificed up to Him, in order that we may begin to desire what He desires. In Luke 14, Jesus urges his followers to count the cost of following him, because to be close to Him, to learn from, and to be used by Him requires us leaving behind everything that our own hearts desire.

In John 6, Jesus feeds the five thousand. It was at this point that Jesus had his greatest following. People love to receive, especially for free. After seeing His miracles, they even try to make Him king (John 6:15.) Then Jesus changes the emphasis of His teaching, He teaches how He, Jesus, is the bread of life, of how everything is held in Him, and of He was sent not to do man's will, but the will of the father. When the people hear this, they begin to grumble, and then to stop following Him (John 6:66.)

People are happy to follow someone who gives them things, such as food, or healing, and indeed Jesus does do this. To give something away to people that they want, or to promise them something that they want is the easiest way to get a following. Promise people healing and you will gain many followers and church members. However, most of the people who followed Jesus up to this point only followed because of what they could get from him, not because of Him. It is this giving away part of Jesus that we like to sell in church, because it does attract followers, the same now as it did then. We can make ourselves a "success" in ministry if only we give the people what they want.

Although Jesus does give us these good things, His healing and His provision are important, His message is more than that. Healing and provision are a natural fruit of walking with Him. However, His message is not about physical bread, but spiritual bread, not just physical life, but the life in Him. It was this change of preaching from the physical to the spiritual that meant many turned away, because the people were only after the physical, they were not interested in the bread of life, but in their own stomachs, they did not want Him, but what he could give them. The hearts of His followers was exposed when He began preaching that He Himself was the real bread.

The 12 disciples did not leave Jesus. They knew that Jesus held the words of life, that He was life (John 6:67.) They had left everything to follow Him, not to get from him, but to be with Him for who he is.

Sacrifice is not an optional extra to our following Jesus, it is the core of His message, both His sacrifice for us, and our sacrifice in order to know and follow Him.

Ascending the Hill of the Lord

"Many peoples will come and say, "Come, let us go up to the mountain of the Lord, to the temple of the God of Jacob. He will teach us his ways, so that we may walk in his paths." (Isaiah 2:3.)

The symbolism of mountains is used many times in the Bible to represent our meeting with God, such as when Moses met God on Mount Sinai, or when Solomon built the Temple on Mount Moriah. Like everything in the Bible, there is a depth of meaning and understanding to be gained by God's use of mountains.

Mountains are absolutely unshakable. they are the most solid, unmovable object in the world. In the above verse from Isaiah, we are told that it is our responsibility to ascend. the mountain to meet God. A mountain, immovable as it is, will never bow down to us, will never compromise, or bow to our will. Jesus has the same character as a mountain, hence him being called the "rock." (Matthew 16:18, 2 Sam 22:3,) Understanding this immovable, solid character of God is vital to understanding who He is, and our relationship with Him.

God instructs His people to travel up the mountain in order to meet Him, Note that the emphasis is on us to travel up to Him. We live in a very "us" focused society. We are used to things being done for us, on our terms. Even our churches often compromise to make God more acceptable to us and to what we think is right. When planning the worship, we often concern ourselves with what man will find acceptable, rather than what God finds acceptable. However, God is a rock, there is no compromise in Him, no submission to what we think is right. the emphasis is put on our responsibility to travel to Him, not the other way round. If we are to really meet with Him, we must do it on His terms, not on ours.

Understanding God as a rock changes our way of thinking, it changes it from thinking that God follows us around, getting involved in what we are doing, to one of us having to turn to God's will, to submit to it, to do things on His terms, His way. It is us who have to travel to Him, His way, not our way.

He wants us to travel to Him, so He can teach us His ways, so that we might follow Him, be able to walk with Him and understand Him. The whole point of everything that has happened in creation, in history and the Bible can be summed up like this: God wants us to be close to Him, to walk with Him and to know Him personally. This is why he tells us to travel to Him, so that we might KNOW him. Knowing about God is not enough. We can study all the books about God, hear all the sermons, know the Bible intimately, and yet that is not a substitute for our own relationship and walk with Him. Hearing what others have learned from God is not enough. As useful and desirable as it is to study and have head knowledge, it never replaces relationship. We need to know Him for ourselves. he wants to teach us His ways himself. We are not to live off somebody else's revelation of Jesus, we must have our own.

'But the Advocate, the Holy Spirit, whom the Father will send in my name, will teach you all things and will remind you of everything I have said to you.' (John 14:26.)

Although God says He wants to teach us His ways himself, teachers are still important, in fact Paul mentions them as part of the Five-fold ministry in Ephesians 4:11. However, we must understand what a teacher should be. A true teacher should not simply pass on their knowledge to us. It may be revelation in the teacher, but passed onto the student, it will just be cold theology. True teaching must always point the student up to the mountain for themselves, it points the way, or enables the student to go to the mountain for themselves, so that the student in turn can go even further than the teacher. True teaching is not simply passing on information or theology, or ways or methods. true teaching is there to enable the student to walk with God themselves Any teaching that is just a formula for "how to do" or that leads the learner to be dependent upon the teacher, or upon method or upon any strength other than Jesus himself is a perversion of what teaching should be . More than just giving information, a good teacher also disciples a student, to see them develop as a person, that they may become that whole person, not a just a person with head knowledge.

True teachers leads to Jesus, they do not try to replace Jesus. There have been many powerful moves of God in His church over the years. They all started with one, or a handful of people who gave themselves over to seeking God and His will. These people's relationship with God led to mighty revivals, such as the Welsh revival of 1904. However, revivals always peter out eventually, as man looks to the methods that these pioneers used, as opposed to seeking God in the way that they did. As soon as man tries to establish a pattern or method, at the expense of seeking God, Jesus is not able to move in the same way that He is when He has a person dedicated to His purposes alone, and to seeking His ways.

Even the Bible itself is not a means to an end. Our goal is not just to have knowledge of the Bible and what God says in it, but to understand that the Bible leads to Jesus Himself. The Bible, as vital and true as it is, in not our relationship with God, but it leads the way to a relationship with God. As the old adage says, we seek the God of the Bible, not the Bible of the God. God wants us to be close to Him, not to a book or to great as learning, as useful and as right as that can be - learning is a good thing, but it is not to take the place of our own personal walk with Jesus, our learning and understanding should point the way to that relationship, never replace it. A true teacher will always help point the way to God, not to themselves or to their understand, or even to the methods that God has given them. We in turn can never understand Jesus by just listening to sermons or studying, or seeking out other people's relationship.

We have to travel up the mountain for ourselves. We can sometimes be too reliant upon others, such as a minister or pastor to go to God for us and tell us what God is saying. We do this, because it takes responsibility off of ourselves and puts it onto someone else. However, a good pastor will not simply do everything for us, but their teaching will be to teach us how to be closer for ourselves.

"Who may ascend the mountain of the Lord? Who may stand in his holy place?The one who has clean hands and a pure heart,who does not trust in an idol or swear by a false god." (Psalm 24:3.)

David explains how we travel up the mountain in Psalm 24. He says that travel up the mountain, there are four criteria: Clean hands, a pure heart, not trusting idols and not swearing by a false god. Let's look briefly at each of these areas:

Clean hands. The cleanliness of our hands in the Bible represents the guilt of our sins, or how much blood is on our hands. The first premise to being close to God is accepting our own sin - ie everything that we do outside of God, and accept Jesus' forgiveness. It is also about our current situation with God. There is no condemnation for our sins, but that doesn't mean that we act however we want. With freedom comes responsibility. We have the freedom to sin, but also have understand the responsibility of how it affects our walk with God and our intimacy with Him. The more we walk in His holiness (as opposed to our own self-righteousness,) the closer we walk with Him.

Pure heart. Our hearts are our desires. A pure heart is simply about what or who we desire. Intimacy with God is a result of our desiring Him. Desiring Him is not the same as desiring the things of Him, (as demonstrated at the feeding of the five thousand,) it's not the same as desiring a ministry, or for Him to move, or to see healing even, as good as those things are, they are the fruits of our relationship with Him, not the goal. As soon as they become the goal, they become idols. A pure heart cares nothing for itself, or for what it can get, or for how it can advance or go further. A pure heart cares only about Him for His sake. A pure heart just wants Him. To know Him. A pure heart will sacrifice everything to simply be close to Him.

"*You will seek me and find me when you seek me with all your heart." (Jer 29:13.)* It says in Jeremiah that we will find Him when we seek Him with all of our hearts. Not just some of our heart, and definitely not when we are seeking the things of Him, as good and as right as those things are, as opposed to seeking Him. Our hearts are key in knowing Jesus, as opposed to knowing about Him. When we desire Him, we will get Him.

Trusting in Idols and swearing by false god's are tied in with having a pure heart. An idol is anything that we trust in rather than God. Anything that comes between our love and trust of Him is an idol. Idol's are often made by the hands of man, and are different from person to person, but we all have them. Our trust needs to be in Him alone.

Swearing by false gods is similar. Swearing by it means putting our promises or faith in something that is not Him, but that sets itself up to be important, or desire to replace the role of Jesus in our lives. Again, these false god's differ according to our own weaknesses. Put simply, though it is trusting in anything that believes itself to be above the power of Jesus.

To draw nearer to Him, the emphasis is put on us to surrender our desires, our lives, our ambitions, everything, and to simply desire one thing - Him. Not the things of Him, we do not seek God's hand, ie what He can do, but we seek His face, who is, His character, His being. The act of doing these things are actually true worship. True worship leads us up His mountain.

The further we travel up His mountain, though that journey of sacrifice and surrender the clearer we will hear Him, and see the truth around us. Places of military authority, such as a castle or army base are always built on the highest point, because from that point you have the clearest view of your surroundings and situation. The further you are up Jesus' mountain, the clearer we can discern what is true and what is false. From outside of His presence, we cannot tell what is or isn't Him. We can try to discern in the flesh, but that does not leads to truth, only to deception and division. The closer we are to Him, the more we will know when someone is speaking from Him, or from their own flesh or understanding, as opposed to God's. He is the only truth ,and we only know that truth through intimacy with Him. The higher up the mountain we are, the more Kingdom authority we walk in.

"Therefore, I urge you, brothers and sisters, in view of God's mercy, to offer your bodies as a living sacrifice, holy and pleasing to God—this is your true and proper worship. Do not conform to the pattern of this world, but be transformed by the renewing of your mind. Then you will be able to test and approve what God's will is—his good, pleasing and perfect will." (Romans 12:1-2.)

Paul states in this verse, if we are to know the will of God, we must sacrifice ourselves first, an echo of what God says in Isaiah 2:3.

The responsibly is upon us to become seeker of Him. Again, not seekers of His works, or miracles, or revival, as good as all those things are, they are the fruit of our knowing Him, not the goal. the goal is Him alone. We must learn to go and meet Him on His terms, His way. It is no coincidence that God told Solomon to build the temple on top of a mountain. He wanted His people to travel to Him, to sacrifice themselves to meet Him on His terms, exactly like he showed His people through the establishing of Moses' tabernacle.

Unity In the Spirit

"Make every effort to keep the unity of the Spirit through the bond of peace. There is one body and one Spirit, just as you were called to one hope when you were called; one

Lord, one faith, one baptism; one God and Father of all, who is over all and through all and in all". (Eph 4:3-6.)

When the people met to pray and worship in the New Testament, the other activity that they entered into was fellowship. His house, as well as being all that we have looked at, should also be a place of unity, of true fellowship.

In a place that is not given over to the work of the Spirit, we can try to manufacture the good and right things of God in the flesh. We can try to force unity through our plans, yet we will never achieve true unity outside of our unity with Jesus. If our meetings with others are not given over to the work of the Spirit, we will not be in unity with Jesus, and we will never be in unity with each other. True unity is a beautiful thing, and major part of God's work, yet if we do not allow spirit-led worship in our lives, we will never achieve unity with each other, we will always be divided by our different viewpoints, agendas or desires.

Jesus is the only truth at any point in time, or in any situation. What He is doing, saying, thinking, is what is truth. Everything else is wrong. Every other opinion, decision, thought, etc, that He is not doing is incorrect, because He is the definition of truth. *(john 14:6)*

Therefore, wherever there is division amongst God's people, it is not because of Jesus, but us. Each one of us has an opinion, a desire, a hope, a dream etc. Most of us operate, and are driven by those wills most of the time, even within the church. One has a desire to set this up, one has a desire to work one way, one has a desire for power, one has a desire to be left alone, one for money, one for success, one to be busy, one for peace and quiet etc.... This is our sinful, self-based nature, our desire to do what we want to do, our way. Sometimes this desire can even be for ministry, or to set up ministries or outreaches. Just because it is a "Christian" based desire, it does not necessarily make it and more righteous, or mean that it is Him that is doing it. A desire is only righteous if it comes from the Righteous One Himself.

There are so many different desires and beliefs within us all, that these inevitably lead to conflict. From major world conflicts between different religions, beliefs or nationality questions, through to conflicts in the home between couples or children, to clashes in workplaces, right through to division both between and within churches. the causes of all of these conflicts is our sin, our selfish desire.

"What causes fights and quarrels among you? Don't they come from your desires that battle within you?.." (James 4:1.)

All these division come because of us following our internal desire for what we want, from a very small scale, to a very big scale. Our "self" or sin causes division. We are driven by what we think is right, and by what we want. That is the sinful nature of man, that he thinks he knows what is best. This is the fruit of eating from the tree of knowledge in the Garden of Eden, this is what sin is - we know best, better than God. It is that drives and motivates our every action and word.

However, at any one point any there is only one true way, one true word or action, and that is what Jesus is saying and doing. If there are 10 people is a room, each will have a different opinion or desire. Some of them may be similar, and they may come to an agreement by majority or by argument, but still there is only one truth - Jesus. Jesus is not democratic. He is not led by the weight of argument, or by man's reasoning (He knows our hearts!) or by what man sees with his eyes. He is a King, and a Kingdom is led by His rule alone. Our job is to find that will, and submit to it. Our job is to be in unison with Him by His Spirit. The church should not be driven by our politics, but by His will. Where two people are united by His Spirit to Him, they will also be united to each other. This is "unity of the Spirit."

It is very important to realise that just because we are a Christian, it does not mean that we know what He is doing or saying at any one point. We only know that the more we lay down ourselves, in order to follow Him. There is a real danger in assuming that just because we are a Christian, His will is the same as our will, and He is behind what we do. It is not Jesus' job to support what we are doing, but our job to become a servant to what Jesus is doing. Jesus does not follow us, we follow Him! Every single church argument, from big to small comes because we assume that our will/way of seeing things is the right way. If we didn't think it wasn't the right way, we wouldn't think it! We must come to the point where we realise how wrong our way of thinking is, how wrong our ambitions are, and how "fallen" our hearts are. Nothing is as deceptive as the human heart (Jer 17:9.) Only when we see that, can we begin to turn away from what we think is right (ie self-righteousness) and start seeking Him and finding out what He is saying, because His opinion is the only truth

The call of a true servant of God is not to seek their own way, but to lay their life down and to seek Jesus' way., in every single area of our life. It is the Holy Spirit that leads us into the truth of Jesus (john 16:13) When we make a conscious decision to lay down our way, and to seek Jesus in every area, it is the Spirit that shows us what He is doing. Being "In the Spirit" is a result of our submission to Jesus, and as a result, the Spirit leads us into unity with Jesus. We can only get in that unity with the Spirit by submission to him and dying to ourselves. the more we get rid of what we think, and turn to Him, the more the Spirit will bring us into union with Him and what he is thinking. As we start or continue our journey of dying to self, the more live in Christ, the clearer we hear Him, the more we desire what He desires, the more we come into synchronisation with Jesus.

There are many passages of the Bible which are about the works of the flesh vs the works of the Spirit. The works of the flesh are the works produced by our own strength, our own wisdom, our own learning, our own theology, and our own will. the works of the Spirit come from our sacrificing what we think is right, and instead seeking His will and His way. It is us truly following Jesus, rather than us leading by our own strength, and then claiming such works to be the works of Jesus.

So Kingdom unity can only be achieved when we are in unity with Him. To the extent that we are in unity with Him, we will be in unity with other genuine servants of God. Jesus is truth, we either align ourselves with that truth in a situation, or we follow our own flesh.

Jesus stated that his real family are the people who do the will of God:*"Who are my mother and my brothers?" he asked. Then he looked at those seated in a circle around him and said, "Here are my mother and my brothers! Whoever does God's will is my brother and sister and mother." (Mark 3:33)*

Jesus did not state that people who held the correct belief, or theology were his family, or those who were Christians or Jews, or those who had an impressive ministry, but rather those who do the will of God. Jesus states that true family unity comes from agreement with God, or to phrase it another way, his family are those who are in unity with God through the Spirit.

The Spirit brings union with Jesus: "Yet a time is coming and has now come when the true worshipers will worship the Father in spirit and truth, for they are the kind of worshipers the Father seeks." (John 4:24)

Jesus states that true worshipers are those who worship in the spirit, ie not out of their flesh, but in submission and agreement with Him. When we worship in the Spirit he takes over our worship, He writes songs though it, speaks though it, intercedes though it. He begins to bring the worship that is in Heaven onto the Earth. That is the worship the father is looking for, worship that is led by Him, not us.

Similarly, Paul stated this:

"And pray in the Spirit on all occasions with all kinds of prayers and requests" (Eph 6:18.)

Paul stated that our praying should be "in the Spirit" not the flesh, ie our praying should be unison with what Jesus is saying and doing, not what we want or think should happen. Again true prayer in the Spirit takes over when we lose our agenda and allow Him to take over. It is not us seeking to get our will done, but us submitting to Jesus and allowing Him to pray through us by His Spirit.

The church will be in true unity only when we are in unity with Him, until then, there will always be division and fighting.

Being in unity, even a little bit (as none of us are completely) brings with it its own conflict. When we are aligned with Jesus' purposes in a situation, it will clash with the will of man. People will want something done one way, and yet Jesus says something different. As we stand for Jesus purpose, the will of man will react against us, often accusing us as we don't do things man's way. Standing for Jesus' will often comes across as arrogant and proud, because there is no compromise in in it. When we are truly standing on the rock, we will not be moved by Man's will. This inevitably leads to clashes and accusation. However, our responsibility is to be so humble to Jesus, so uninterested in our own will that we only care about Him and His ways. this will look arrogant to the world and to those outside of that unity with Him, and yet it is actually the real definition of humility. This is why Jesus said that His coming will not bring peace, but division (Matthew 10:34.) It is also why one of Jesus' many titles is the "Rock of Offence" (1 Peter 2:8) Because Jesus' will and following it is an offence to the world, and unfortunately, often to the church too.

So unity in the Spirit comes from our being in unity with Him. There will always be conflict between those not in unity with the Spirit, and also between those who are in unity with Jesus, and those who aren't, even within the church. It is important to note that none of us are in unity with Jesus all the time, but the more we submit ourselves and seek Him, the more in unity with Him we will be.

We have to be willing to seek and sacrifice ourselves until we are able to walk with Him as closely as we can. This will lead to conflict and accusation both from the world and the church, but as we grow in unison with Him, we grow in true unity with those who are also in unity with Him. My genuine family are those who also seek and long for His will and way, and are willing to lay themselves down to find Him. I have had many encounters with people, sometimes complete strangers who I have known are my true family, and the love and respect I have for them burns with such passion. I know I will know these people for eternity, even if I never get to actually meet them properly here on Earth! This is not a fleshly unity, brought about by my efforts, but a unity brought about by being in Him. Like anything of God, it cannot be counterfeited or achieved by anyone's works or strengths, but by Him and Him alone.

Our earthly unity will only come from our unity with Him. Unity can never be gained by looking at ourselves or each or, or by our schemes, but only by coming into unity with Him by His Spirit. As we restore true worship in our lives and churches, we will also come not just into deeper unity with Him, but also into closer unity to others who are in Him.

Worship in Spirit

"Yet a time is coming and has now come when the true worshipers will worship the Father in spirit and truth, for they are the kind of worshipers the Father seeks". (John 4:23.)

Jesus specifies that true worship is in spirit and truth, which also implies that worship that is not in spirit, is not true worship. So worship, if it is in the Spirit, must not only be for God, but come from God, from His Spirit. Worship cannot be on our terms, it cannot be what we find acceptable to give to God, it has to be done in His truth, or how He ordains, and by His Spirit. For too long, we as Christians have been telling God what we find acceptable, what sort of church service we are willing to attend, what style of music we would like, how long the service should be, what sort of sermon we would like to hear, and so on. The truth is that church is not on our terms. It is not our church, it is His. Jesus says that He will build His church (Matthew 16:18.) It is built by Him, by His Spirit.

Therefore worship is built by Him, His truth, His Spirit. That is the worship Jesus is looking for. To worship in Spirit, we again have to start from a point of brokenness. While we are not broken to the purposes of God, He cannot take over While we try to minister on our own strength, He is not ministering through us. Whenever we act out of our own ability, our own opinions, our own desires, our own ideas, then the Holy Spirit is not building His church, we are trying to build His church for Him, only it will not really be His church, it will be our ministry, and ultimately will not set people free, but chain them into religion. We have to be prepared to give our meetings and services over to Him, not just in word, but in action, too.

True worship, the worship that the Father is looking for, is worship that the Holy Spirit takes over – because it is in that place that people will begin to encounter God. When we look at the analogy of the Tabernacle of Moses, the journey into the presence of God began in the flesh, with singing and dancing, thanksgiving and celebration. To get in the Spirit, we must start off in the flesh. Our worship services should begin with straightforward praise songs, which is what most of our services do anyway. A praise song is loud, bold, triumphant, and focuses on who Jesus is, what He has done, His truth, His victory. Praise is a powerful weapon to clearing the spiritual atmosphere and preparing us to meet with Jesus.

However, as we continue on our journey of sacrifice and surrender, and it is only when we begin to surrender ourselves that the Spirit can begin to take over, and He begins to lead His worship. Remember, without sacrifice, surrender and brokenness, there will be no true Spirit led worship. Worship that remains in the flesh stays in the outer courts, which is fine, but it isn't the true worship that the Father is looking for.

So true worship usually begins in the flesh, through the use of songs, but ends up being taken over by the Spirit. When we worship in the Spirit, we worship in complete unity with Him and what He is doing. Our job is to bring the Kingdom of Heaven onto the earth (Matthew 6:10.) When we are in unity with Him through His Spirit, we are in unity with all that is going on in the Heavens. We can bring the worship of heaven into our meetings, if we are willing to abandon ourselves to seeking Him and His way.

I will try to explain how I try to implement this practically within a service. This is an example from my own life, but, the practicalities and song choices will vary from person to person, from church to church. What does not change, though, is the journey of sacrifice and surrendering, and the openness to allow Him to work though the service.

If I were to lead worship today, I would usually start with a few choruses picked out. For this example, I will only have 3 choruses in my worship session. I will start with a praise song, such songs would be something like, "Hosanna," "Days of Elijah," "Let Everything That Has Breath..." etc. The actual choice of song is obviously up to you, which songs you know and which songs your church uses. It is irrelevant whether it is the latest chorus, or the oldest hymn, but we must understand the difference between praise and a worship song. A praise song is always loud, bold, proclaims God, and exalts Jesus. It is our sacrifice of praise, deciding to proclaim the truth of God, despite how we may feel. Praise songs are just that, songs. They are sung in the flesh, with the purpose of beginning to focus us upon Jesus, our goal. In your service, you may want to use two or even three praise songs. However, it is important that you do not just sing praise songs, because without the Spirit taking over, you will not encounter God as you might otherwise.

The second of a three chorus set will be something that begins to introduce surrender, adoration, the welcoming of Jesus into the service. It is a song where we want to begin to move into the Holy Place. This sort of chorus will usually be slower, more reverential, but importantly either focused upon Jesus, or focused upon dealing with ourselves.

The sort of song I would use here would be something like, "Shout To The Lord, "He is Exalted," or "Majesty." Again, I am picking songs that most people would recognise, but you would use whatever song is appropriate to your church. During the second song, or middle of your worship time, you should be looking at bringing people into that place of submission, into place surrender to the Holy Spirit. You are trying to lead the congregation into focusing entirely upon Jesus, not on themselves or the service, the words, or their surroundings, but upon Him. We should start allowing space in the music for people to worship out of their spirits. We may want to stop singing the song that is written, but keep the music going, and allow people to worship with their own words, or to pray, or to call on God. I try to keep the music going during this time, as it creates continuity, and a flow, but start allowing the Holy Spirit to do what He wants to do.

This leads us into the Holy Place. A place where there is nothing but pure, worship. True worship songs are not sung about Jesus or about the things of God, but to Jesus directly. Worship songs are often very simple, and I find that it doesn't need too many words, as remembering, or focusing upon a lot of words distracts our attention from Him. I am cautious of songs that use too many words, as people end up focusing on getting the words right, or reading a screen whereas if the song is very simple, it is easier to switch off, and focus straight at God. It is for the same reason that I personally am very cautious of "visual aids" in corporate worship, I personally find that they just serve to take our eyes off Jesus, which is the very opposite of what true worship should be.

Our worship songs should be very simple, usually slow or relaxed musically, sometimes powerful, but always just focused upon Jesus. There are many true worship songs, such as, "How great is our God," "Holy, Holy, Holy," Salvation Belongs to Our God, etc. When we worship in a place of true submission, the Holy Spirit will begin to take over our worship. He might start to release prophetic songs, (this is how most of the Psalms were written,) or new songs that you have never heard before. Again, it is important to keep the music going, but do not force the songs upon the people, but rather let songs, be they new, prophetic or songs you already know, rise up from the people and the worship leaders.

Our song choice must have a sense of direction. There must be a clear understanding from the worship leader of what worship is, and where they are leading the people. A worship leader must be both a worshiper and a leader. A leader cannot take other where they themselves cannot go, and so we cannot have worship leaders who are not worshipers. Being a worshiper is the first requirement for any worship leader, but being a leader is the second. If you are leading people, make the route clear. There should be a sense of progression, not just staying with praise, but moving people deeper. The worship leader must always lead the people as far as they can into God's throne room.

Let the Spirit take over, let Him lead you. Do not rush, and do not try to stick to any agenda, allow Him to do what He wants. As you move deeper into God's presence, you give more space to Him to move, by allowing the music to keep moving, and allowing Him to take over. A worship time may start in the flesh, but should always end up in the Spirit. This is where God moves through His people. He can do what He wants, and it will be different with each individual, he may heal people, he may give them revelation, he may call them to repentance, he may move a church into prayer or intercession. We as worship leaders or ministers must get out of the way of what He wants to do. Nothing is more important to God than Him ministering to His people.

The Tabernacle of David - Restoring Worship

"In that day I will restore David's fallen tent. I will repair its broken places, restore its ruins, and build it as it used to be" (Amos 9:11.)

This verse, which is also quoted in Acts 15:16, is vital in understanding God's purpose for worship in these times.

The Tabernacle that David established was different to Moses'. David established a tabernacle, which also housed the Ark of the Covenant. It was where David housed the Ark, for 40 years, until the temple was built, in 964 BC. (See 2 Samuel 6, 1 Chronicles 13-16.) This Tabernacle was different in nature to Moses' tabernacle.

David's tabernacle still housed the Ark, and the Levites still ministered in it. We can see in Chronicles and Samuel, that this tabernacle was a place of great rejoicing, of music, of singing, and of dancing. What is different to Moses' tabernacle, though, was that apart from the Ark, which housed God's presence, it did not house any of the other furniture that Moses had. Moses' tabernacle was essential, in that it was prophetic of what was to come, of Jesus' sacrifice and of the work of the Holy Spirit. David's tabernacle has sometimes been described as a New Testament church in the Old Testament.

The only sacrifice in David's tabernacle was the sacrifice of praise, and the sacrifice of the heart. It was a true centre of worship, with God's presence being in the very midst of His people. Most of the Psalms were written, prophetically in times of worship in the tabernacle. It was a place of true praise and worship, prophecy, encounter, and the fullness of the presence of God. David understood that Moses' tabernacle was prophetic, it showed physically how things are to be done spiritually, and his tabernacle was to be the fulfilment of all that Moses prophesied.

In Amos 9:11, and again in Acts 15, God promises that he will restore David's tabernacle, rebuild it how it used to be. Jesus, and the sending of the Holy Spirit is part of the fulfilment of this prophecy, because without His sacrifice, and the Spirit, it would be impossible to see David's tabernacle restored as it was. That is what God is looking to do in our churches, restore David's tabernacle, to see them become places full of Holy Spirit led worship. They should be places full of joy, rejoicing, dancing and celebration. The presence of God should be the centre of all that goes on there.

I also believe that this prophecy speaks to His church in the present day, that it is David's tabernacle He is restoring. Where our churches have allowed religion and resistance to the purposes of God, He is restoring David's fallen tent, that place of unadulterated presence and glory. When we look at any revival that has happened in history, they have been times of outpouring, where His Spirit, His will, and His glory dominate, which transforms the lives of the people. That is how God sees His church, as it was in David's time.

We must also remember that God is not just talking about physical places when he talks of the tabernacle today, he is also talking about us, His temple. We are the house of His Spirit, and it is our lives that should be so open to Him and what He is doing, whether we be on our own, or when we meet with others.

Wineskins

"And no one pours new wine into old wineskins. Otherwise, the new wine will burst the skins; the wine will run out and the wineskins will be ruined." (Luke 5:37.)

When Jesus spoke about wineskins, He was again talking about us, the temples of God, the carriers of His presence. In order for us to accept the new, the deep and the magnificent work that God wants to do in our lives, we have to get rid of some of our old way of thinking and doing. We cannot simply add what God is doing on top of what we are already doing, as this verse states, we will end up being damaged. In order to accept what it is that he wants to do both in our lives and in our churches, we are going to have to have new wineskin mentality.

In practical terms, that means that we have to let go of our old thinking and ways of operating, and allow ourselves to be open to what He wants to do. Man finds comfort in the familiar, and our wineskins soon become old and inflexible. This is how all the past revivals petered out, what starts out as Spirit soon falls into man's routine. The new wineskin becomes the old, and is incapable of receiving the new that God has for us.

If we are to become the bride that Jesus is preparing, then we are going to have to leave some of our old systems behind. It is not wrong to continue in those ways, as such, but it will mean that we are not open, and will therefore miss the new that God has for us. If we continue as we always have, we will continue have what we've always had.

To be a new wineskin, we must get rid of any agenda that we have, and come back to seeking His face. We have to be carriers of His presence, not carriers of our own agenda. Our flesh will never transform us or those that we have contact with. His Spirit will.

This is what is what God is calling His church back to in this time. Indeed we can see it starting to take place in churches throughout the world, places which are given over to 24 hour praise and worship. This is a part of what God is doing in this age, returning His bride to Him, and rebuilding David's fallen tent.

Worship within the Church

We need to apply the spiritual lessons of Moses' and David's tabernacles to our church worship today. We also need to understand why we use music in our worship, and how to use that music to draw people into God's presence.

So what role does music have in worship? Music is not worship. The two things are distinct from each other. Just because a person is singing a song with the words Jesus in, it does not necessarily mean that they are worshiping Jesus. Indeed, there are many different types of Christian songs, all of which are valid, such as songs for evangelism, songs that teach, songs that inspire, and this is correct and proper. However, in this booklet, we are looking specifically at songs designed to lead us into God's presence.

Worship can only come from our hearts. Non musical people can worship just as well as musical people. We often make a mistake in our churches by getting the best (or only) musicians to lead worship in our churches, whereas we should be getting people who are first and foremost worshipers. Too many people assume that they cannot worship, because they are not great singers or musicians, and also assume that a person can worship because they are a great musician. Musical ability, and a worshiping heart are completely unrelated to each other. We need to change our thinking on the correlation between music and worship, or it will hinder our own worship, and our churches worship.

What music does do, though, is express our worship. Music is not the worship itself, but the expression from our heart. Music is a powerful tool, and it is only a tool, but it has the ability to convey and carry the worship from one person's heart into a much larger space. When one person is worshiping, music has the ability to carry other people along with the worship, if used skilfully and knowledgeably, to help to lead a congregation of people into true worship, and then into the presence of God. That is why it is vital for a worshiper leader (i.e. someone who leads others into worship, as opposed to a worshiper, which we are all called to be, but we don't have the responsibility to lead others,) to understand music, because it is their tool, it is the weapon that they use to take the people along to the place that he or she must go to in their own time in a corporate setting.

So music is a tool, a tool by which a worshiper can lead other people into worship. It is a tool to express one's own worshiping heart and place of worship. That is the power of music

For those who are called to lead God's people in worship, it is right that we become excellent musicians, because music is our tool to lead the people. We must know how to use this tool skilfully. However, the tool is useless unless we can learn to walk in brokenness and surrender to the Spirit of God. In the same way that we wouldn't ask someone off the streets to preach in our church just because they are a great public speaker, we shouldn't be asking people to lead worship just because they are a great singer or musician. We can see how important the worship should be in our services, and the job of leading people into God's presence should not be given out lightly.

As I previously mentioned, the worship leader, or indeed anyone leading in our churches, including the ministers, must be worshipers first and foremost. If we are not worshipers, we will never be in unity with Jesus via His Spirit. We will simply minister out of our gifts, but in the flesh. This will not be kingdom, but religion, not matter how impressive it may look. If anyone who is a leader within our churches are not a worshiper, than they will never lead the people the right way. The first characteristic of every single person of God in the Bible was that inspite of the fact they were not perfect, or were occasionally rebellious, they always returned to seeking and obeying God's heart. Having rebellion or pride in our hearts is not in itself an issue, as we all do, but the inability to recognise it and to be prepared to seek His heart and be changed, is an issue.

If a leader in any role is not able to constantly humble themselves and go back to Him to seek His way, then they will lead the people the wrong way. Jesus is the way. the narrow path is so narrow, the only way to remain on it is to walk in submission to Him, in that state of worship that Paul talks about in Romans 12.

If we have our services led merely by people who are talented in their flesh, then our meetings will only have the things of the flesh, but in a spiritual guise. Our worship leaders, pastors, ministers, and every other role must be worshipers first, without that, we will never have God's heart, and we will never walk in true Kingdom authority and anointing. If we cannot humble ourselves before the King, all that we produce will only ever lead men to us and what we are building. A genuine worshiper is happy to be the last, to lead men to Jesus.

True fruit is only produced as a result of intimacy with the Father. When a man and woman are in love, out of their love they will be intimate, and of that intimacy, children will be produced. The children are a result of the intimacy. So it is with Jesus. Our private, unseen intimacy will produce genuine fruit in our lives, the fruit of His Spirit. We cannot produce these without the intimacy. Without the intimacy, we will not produce fruit, we will have to counterfeit it by in our flesh.

Until we give our lives and meetings back to Him and His leadership, we will never become what we are called to be. The ways of the flesh are easier to control, we can build by our own resources, we can establish our own paths relatively easily. The way the of the Spirit, however, requires our giving up control, surrendering all our desire, plans and ambitions, and looking to Him. Our flesh would organise God out of our lives and services, but if we learned to humble ourselves, seek His face, pray and repent, then He would hear from heaven, forgive our wicked ways and heal our land.

Until we learn to walk in unity with Jesus, through our hearts being changed in worship, no area of God's body will be able to function as it should. Without connection to the head, an arm or a leg is useless. So it is with the parts of God's body, His church. Each function of the church has to be in unity with the head, whether that is evangelism, teaching, prophecy or so on. Without being in unity with Him, we will walk in our callings, but in the flesh, in our authority, not in His. This is why it is so essential that we restore worship back to its' proper place, in order to operate effectively as a church. Until we restore that true heart of worship, the whole body will not be able to function correctly.

The Kingdom of God cannot begin to advance while we are still operating in our own strength, ability and desires. Ministry that is not in His Spirit, in unity with Him, is not real ministry, but our works. We must turn ourselves back to the core of what Christianity is, to deny ourselves and to follow Him. When we as His people learn to walk in this reality, we will impact this world in a way never seen before. These are the times we are in, and this is what God is doing with His church, purifying us and preparing us for His coming. Let us turn our hearts back to the King.

Made in the USA
Lexington, KY
30 October 2014